Piano • Vocal • Guitar

Songs from

Cover and Interior Photos: Andy Hutch

ISBN 0-7935-9542-8

HAL•LEONARD®
CORPORATION

7777 W. BLUEMOUND RD. P.O. BOX 13819 MILWAUKEE, WI 53213

Visit Hal Leonard Online at
www.halleonard.com

Songs from
cuttingedge

delirious?

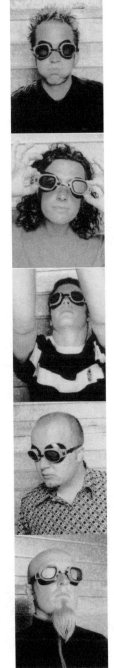

contents

5	All I Want Is You
12	Did You Feel The Mountains Tremble?
22	Find Me In The River
28	The Happy Song
44	I Could Sing Of Your Love Forever
56	I'm Not Ashamed
37	I've Found Jesus
66	Lord, You Have My Heart
70	Louder Than The Radio
49	Message Of The Cross
76	Obsession
84	Shaken Up
90	Singers Song
98	Thank You For Saving Me
105	What Is This Thing Called Love?

cutting edge

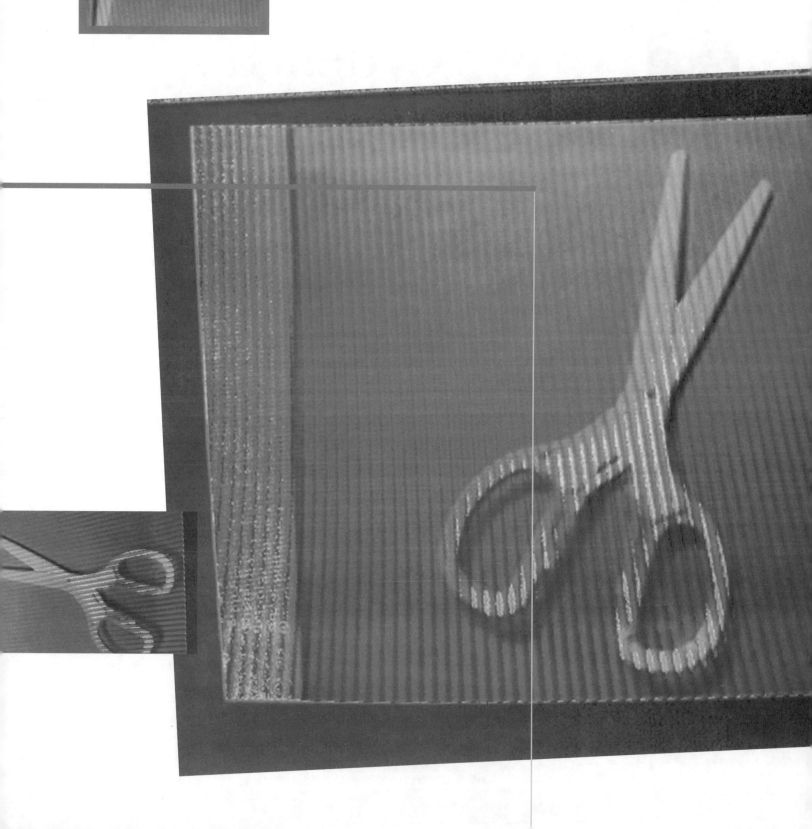

All I Want Is You

Words and Music by
MARTIN SMITH

Did You Feel The Mountains Tremble?

Words and Music by
MARTIN SMITH

Did you feel, _____ did you

21

Find Me In The River

Words and Music by
MARTIN SMITH

Find me in the riv - er;
suf-f'ring,

The Happy Song

Words and Music by
MARTIN SMITH

Fast two-beat

Oh, I could sing un - end - ing
I could sing dance a thou - sand

Solo ends

cel - e - brate, hey, for joy is in ___ this

place. *Vocal 1st time only*
Instrumental solo - ad lib.

Oh, ___ I could sing un -

Solo ends

I've Found Jesus

Words and Music by
MARTIN SMITH

I Could Sing Of Your Love Forever

Words and Music by
MARTIN SMITH

Lyrics:

O - ver the moun-tains and the sea Your riv-er runs with love for me, and I will o-pen up my heart and let the Heal-er set me free. I'm hap-py to be in the truth and I will dai-ly lift my hands, for I will al-ways sing of when Your love came down, yeah.

Message Of The Cross

Words and Music by
MARTIN SMITH

This is the mes-sage of ___ the

I'm Not Ashamed

Words and Music by
MARTIN SMITH

Was a time ___ as a lit - tle boy ___ when I ___
There were times ___ in my bar - ren - ness ___ when I ___

___ said I'd ___ fol - low You,
___ felt your ___ pure af - fec - tion

shamed an-y-more, __

'cause I've felt the oil _____ pour down __ o-ver me.

for you,   on - ly ___ for you. ___

Play   like you're not   a - shamed, _   hey!

Lord, You Have My Heart

Words and Music by
MARTIN SMITH

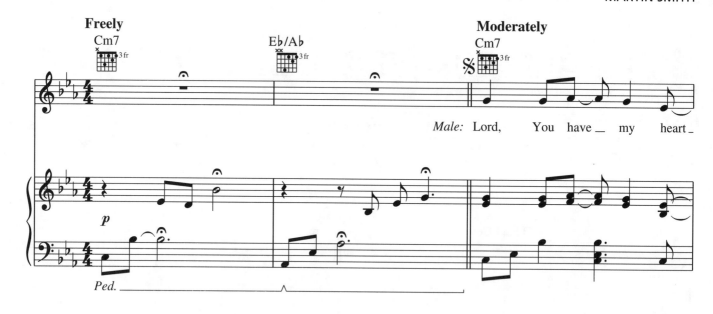

Male: Lord, You have __ my heart __

__ and I will search __ for Yours. __

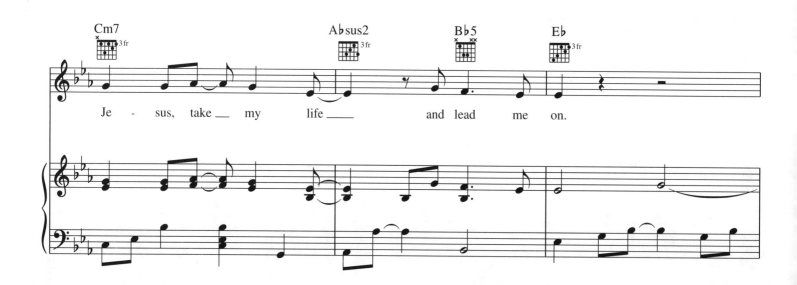

Je - sus, take __ my life ___ and lead me on.

Louder Than The Radio

Words and Music by
MARTIN SMITH

Obsession

Words and Music by
MARTIN SMITH

Slow, heavy feel

N.C.

mf

What can I do with my ob - ses-sion,
And I'm so filth - y with my sin.

with the things I can-not see? ____
I car - ry pride like a dis-ease. _

And my heart, _

Shaken Up

Words and Music by
MARTIN SMITH

88

Singers Song

Words and Music by
MARTIN SMITH

Thank You For Saving Me

Words and Music by
MARTIN SMITH

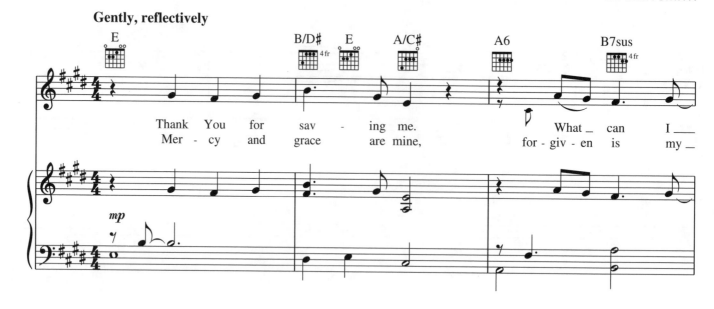

Thank You for sav - ing me.
What __ can I __

Mer - cy and grace are mine,
for - giv - en is my __

__ say?
You are my ev - 'ry - thing.

__ sin.
Je - sus my on - ly home,

I will sing Your praise.
You shed Your

the Sav - iour of the world.
"Great is the

What Is This Thing Called Love?

Words and Music by
MARTIN SMITH